I Found You

Mrigendra Bharti

Published by Sellbrochure Vymish Entertainment, 2024.

I FOUND YOU

First edition. June 18, 2024.

ISBN: 979-8227572042

Written by Mrigendra Bharti.

Table of Contents

Preface

As I present to you this collection, "I Found You," I am filled with immense joy and inspiration. This anthology of poems delves into the profound and intricate world of love, capturing the essence of finding that special someone who brings light to life. Each poem in this book tells a story of love – sometimes filled with joy, sometimes touched by sorrow, and often marked by a blissful serenity. Through each word, each vivid image, and every rhythmic cadence, I aim to convey the multifaceted nature of love and the profound impact of discovering that one person who makes everything complete.

"I Found You" is dedicated to all those who have experienced the magic of finding their soulmate, the one who understands the unspoken, who brings comfort in chaos, and whose presence turns ordinary moments into extraordinary memories. My hope is that these poems will resonate with your heart, reflecting the depth of your own experiences and emotions.

Thank you for embarking on this journey with me. May these verses bring you as much joy in reading as they brought me in writing.

Prologue

Love is an eternal quest, a journey that takes us through uncharted territories of the heart. It is a force that transcends time, space, and reason, binding us to those who touch our souls in the most profound ways. "I Found You" is a collection of poems that captures the essence of this timeless journey — the exhilarating moment of discovery when two hearts recognize each other in a crowded world.

In these verses, I have sought to encapsulate the myriad emotions that accompany the experience of finding that special someone. Each poem is a testament to the beauty of connection, the thrill of new beginnings, and the depth of enduring love. From the first spark of attraction to the quiet comfort of companionship, these poems celebrate the transformative power of love.

As you turn these pages, you will encounter stories of joy and sorrow, hope and longing, passion and tranquility. These poems are not just words on paper; they are echoes of the heart, reflections of the soul, and tributes to the people who inspire us to love deeply and live fully.

"I Found You" is an invitation to immerse yourself in the magic of love's discovery. May these poems resonate with your own experiences and remind you of the beauty and wonder of finding that one person who completes your story.

Welcome to "I Found You." May your heart find its own echoes in these words and may you cherish the love that they seek to celebrate.

Introduction

Love, in its many forms, has always been a source of inspiration and wonder. It is the thread that weaves through our lives, connecting us to each other and to the deeper parts of ourselves. "I Found You" is a collection born from this universal experience, celebrating the profound impact of finding that special person who transforms our world.

This book is a journey through the landscape of love, told in the language of poetry. Each poem is a snapshot of moments that capture the essence of discovering and cherishing a meaningful connection. Whether it's the first flutter of attraction, the comfort of shared silence, or the joy of mutual understanding, these verses reflect the myriad emotions that love brings into our lives.

The poems in "I Found You" are deeply personal yet universally relatable. They explore the highs and lows, the certainty and the doubts, the dreams and the realities of loving and being loved. Through these words, I hope to convey the beauty and complexity of love, and to offer a space where readers can see their own experiences reflected and validated.

This collection is dedicated to those who have found their special someone, as well as those who are still searching. It is a tribute to the journey of love, with all its twists and turns, its moments of clarity and its mysteries. I invite you to read these poems with an open heart and to let them resonate with your own story.

Thank you for joining me on this poetic journey. May "I Found You" bring you joy, comfort, and inspiration, and may you find within its pages the echoes of your own heart.

Connect With Mrigendra,
Thank you very much for choosing this book.
You can also connect with me on Instagram,
https://www.instagram.com/i_mrigendrabharti.official
With Love,
Mrigendra Bharti

Her Enchanting Essence

Her eyes, a galaxy of dreams untold,
In their depths, countless stories unfold.
They shimmer like stars in the midnight sky,
Drawing me in, making me high.
Her voice, a melody, so soft and sweet,
Every word she utters, a cherished treat.
It dances through the air, light as a feather,
Binding my heart, forever tethered.
Her unique grace, a sight to behold,
With every move, a new story is told.
Her laughter, a song, pure and bright,
Chasing away the darkest night.
Her hair, a cascade, wild and free,
Flowing like waves of the endless sea.
Each strand, a thread of liquid gold,
In their sway, a tale of love is told.
Her smile, a beacon, warm and true,
In its glow, my world finds its hue.
It lights up my life, every single day,
Guiding me through, come what may.
Though my love remains, a silent prayer,
In every glance, her essence I wear.
A one-sided love, pure and deep,
In my heart, her memories I keep.

Her Eyes
Her eyes, like twilight's gentle embrace,
In their depths, my heart finds its place.
Emerald pools of unspoken dreams,
Where every glance with passion teems.

Her Voice
Her voice, a whisper, soft and pure,
A melody that I adore.
Each word, a note, in a love song,
In her presence, I belong.

Her Grace
Her grace, unmatched, a rare delight,
With every move, she ignites the night.
An elegance, both wild and tame,
In her sway, I find no shame.

Her Hair
Her hair, a river of silken threads,
Flowing gently, as the daylight spreads.
Each strand, a story, a golden hue,
In its flow, my love feels true.

Her Smile
Her smile, a sunrise in the gloom,
Lighting up the darkest room.
A curve of joy, pure and bright,
In its warmth, I find my light.

Her Laughter
Her laughter, a song, light and free,
An echo of pure, blissful glee.
It rings through the air, clear and bright,
Chasing away the darkest night.

Her Presence

Her eyes, a universe of dreams untold,
In their depths, countless stories unfold.
Emerald pools of unspoken grace,
In their gaze, my heart finds its place.
Her voice, a whisper through the gentle breeze,
A melody that sets my soul at ease.
Every word she utters, a soft refrain,
Binding my heart in a tender chain.
Her laughter, a song, light and free,
An echo of pure, blissful glee.
It rings through the air, clear and bright,
Chasing away the darkest night.
Her hair, a cascade of silken threads,
Flowing gently, like the daylight spreads.
Each strand, a ray of golden light,
In its touch, my love takes flight.
Her smile, a beacon in the storm,
A warmth that keeps my heart so warm.
A curve of joy, so bright and true,
In its light, my dreams renew.
Her presence, a serene, calming sea,
In her aura, I find tranquility.
A silent strength, both soft and strong,
In her company, I belong.

Though unspoken, my love does grow,
In every glance, it starts to show.
A one-sided love, pure and deep,
In my heart, her memories I keep.

Her Radiance

In her presence, my world finds light,
Her radiance, a beacon in the night.
With every glance, my heart takes flight,
Enraptured by her beauty bright.
Her eyes, two pools of endless grace,
Reflecting depths I long to trace.
In their depths, I find solace,
Lost in their enchanting embrace.
Her voice, a melody, sweet and clear,
Whispering secrets only I can hear.
Each word she speaks, a symphony rare,
Filling my soul with tender care.
Her laughter, like music to my ears,
Dispelling all my doubts and fears.
In its sound, pure joy appears,
Echoing through the passing years.
Her smile, a curve that lights the way,
Guiding me through each passing day.
With every beam, my worries sway,
In its warmth, I long to stay.
Her presence, a sanctuary divine,
Where troubles fade and spirits shine.
In her company, I find peace,
A refuge from life's ceaseless cease.

Forever in awe of her wondrous grace,
In her love, I find my rightful place.
With each passing moment, my heart yearns,
For her, my love forever burns.

Glimpse of Grace

In her glimpse, a moment divine,
A sight so rare, it makes time unwind.
With just one look, my heart takes flight,
Enthralled by her beauty, pure and bright.
Her eyes, like jewels, sparkle and gleam,
Reflecting a world where dreams redeem.
In their depths, I see galaxies dance,
Lost in their enchanting trance.
Her smile, a curve that lights up the sky,
A beacon of hope when days run dry.
With every grin, my worries subside,
In its glow, my fears collide.
Her laughter, a melody, sweet and clear,
A symphony that I hold dear.
In its sound, my soul finds peace,
As troubles and sorrows cease.
Her presence, a blessing, a gift untold,
A sanctuary where love unfolds.
With every step, she graces the earth,
A vision of grace, of infinite worth.
In her glimpse, I find my salvation,
A glimpse of heaven, a divine sensation.
With every sight, my love does grow,
For her, my heart beats, aglow.

Celestial Glance

In her glance, the stars align,
A celestial wonder, pure and fine.
Her eyes, two orbs of radiant light,
Turning the day from dark to bright.
Her voice, a serenade of dreams,
Like gentle whispers of flowing streams.
Each note she utters, a spell so sweet,
Making my heart skip its beat.
Her hair, like waves of silken night,
Flows in cascades, soft and bright.
A golden halo, a crown so fair,
In its shimmer, I find my prayer.
Her touch, a whisper of the breeze,
A gentle caress that puts me at ease.
In her embrace, my world finds peace,
All burdens and fears find release.
Her smile, a dawn of endless grace,
Illuminates the darkest space.
With every beam, my spirit lifts,
In its warmth, I find life's gifts.
Her presence, a calm, serene and true,
A guiding light in all I do.
In her company, my soul feels free,
In her love, my destiny.

Her Radiant Glance

Her glance, a sunrise in my soul,
A radiant light that makes me whole.
Her eyes, a dance of moonlit beams,
Turning reality into dreams.
Her voice, a gentle lullaby,
A soothing breeze as night goes by.
Each word she speaks, a tender grace,
Envelops me in warm embrace.
Her laughter, a cascading stream,
Pure joy that glows with a golden gleam.
In its sound, I find my bliss,
A melody I cannot miss.
Her hair, a waterfall of gold,
Flowing freely, stories untold.
Each strand, a thread of light,
Weaving dreams throughout the night.
Her smile, a spark of divine light,
Guides me through the darkest night.
With every curve, my heart does soar,
In its glow, I yearn for more.
Her presence, a gentle balm,
In her aura, I find calm.
With every moment spent with her,
Life becomes a gentle blur.

Angelic Presence

In her presence, angels sing,
A divine melody they bring.
Her eyes, a mirror of the skies,
Reflecting love that never dies.
Her voice, a harp of golden strings,
Echoes with the joy she brings.
Each syllable, a note of grace,
Filling my heart with her embrace.
Her laughter, a symphony bright,
A chorus of pure, shining light.
In its sound, I find my song,
A melody where I belong.
Her hair, a river of silk so fine,
Flows with a grace that is divine.
Each strand, a story, pure and true,
A golden thread in morning dew.
Her smile, a beacon in the storm,
Radiates a warmth, pure and warm.
With every beam, my world transforms,
In its light, love's essence forms.
Her presence, a serene embrace,
A sanctuary of endless grace.
In her aura, my spirit's free,
In her love, eternity.

Divine Radiance

Her eyes, like stars in the midnight sky,
Sparkle with a grace that makes me sigh.
Deep within, a universe resides,
A world of wonder that never hides.
Her voice, a melody so pure,
A soothing balm, a gentle cure.
Each word she speaks, a note of bliss,
A symphony I can't resist.
Her laughter, a joyful chime,
Ringing through the sands of time.
In its echo, I find delight,
A sound that makes my world bright.
Her hair, a cascade of midnight silk,
Flows with a grace that's pure and ilk.
Each strand, a thread of golden light,
Dancing in the moonlit night.
Her smile, a beacon in the storm,
Radiates a warmth that keeps me warm.
A curve of joy, a spark of grace,
In its glow, my heart finds its place.
Her presence, a serene embrace,
A sanctuary of endless grace.
With her, my soul finds peace,
In her love, my dreams increase.

Ethereal Charm

Her eyes, a glimpse of the divine,
In their depths, the stars align.
Gazing into their emerald hue,
I see a world that's pure and true.
Her voice, a whisper on the breeze,
A melody that puts my heart at ease.
Each word, a gentle lullaby,
A song that lifts my spirits high.
Her laughter, a cascading stream,
Filling my world with a golden gleam.
In its sound, pure joy I find,
A melody that soothes my mind.
Her hair, a river of silken light,
Flows like the dawn breaking the night.
Each strand, a ray of sunlit gold,
In its touch, a story told.
Her smile, a dawn of endless grace,
Illuminates the darkest space.
With every curve, my soul does soar,
In its light, I yearn for more.
Her presence, a calming sea,
In her aura, I find tranquility.
A gentle strength, both soft and true,
In her company, my spirit flew.

Serene Elegance

Her eyes, two orbs of liquid light,
Shine with a brilliance, pure and bright.
In their depths, a world I see,
A place where my heart longs to be.
Her voice, a gentle serenade,
A melody that will never fade.
Each note she sings, a touch of grace,
Filling my heart with her embrace.
Her laughter, a song of pure delight,
A sound that makes my soul take flight.
In its echo, joy I find,
A melody that's intertwined.
Her hair, a waterfall of silk,
Flows with a grace that's pure as milk.
Each strand, a whisper of the dawn,
A golden thread to which I'm drawn.
Her smile, a beacon in the dark,
A flame that lights my inner spark.
With every beam, my world ignites,
In its glow, my heart delights.
Her presence, a serene retreat,
A place where my soul feels complete.
In her aura, peace I find,
A sanctuary for heart and mind.

Timeless Beauty

In her eyes, the dawn does break,
A gentle light, for my heart's sake.
Emerald pools of endless grace,
Where dreams and reality interlace.
Her voice, a melody divine,
Each word a note that does entwine.
It weaves through air, a tender kiss,
A song of love, eternal bliss.
Her laughter, a bell of joy untold,
Ringing with a warmth, pure gold.
It brightens days, a radiant gleam,
An echo of a perfect dream.
Her hair, a cascade of moonlit night,
Flowing with a soft, gentle light.
Each strand a river of silken thread,
In its sway, my heart is led.
Her smile, a burst of morning sun,
Radiates joy, touches everyone.
With every curve, my soul does rise,
In its warmth, a paradise.
Her presence, a calm, serene and pure,
In her embrace, I find my cure.
A sanctuary, a place of peace,
Where all my troubles find release.

Angelic Aura

Her eyes, twin stars that light my way,
Guide me through night, into the day.
In their depths, I see my dreams,
A world of wonder, where love redeems.
Her voice, a whisper on the wind,
A gentle breeze where dreams begin.
Each syllable, a touch of grace,
A melody I can't erase.
Her laughter, a song so sweet,
A joyous rhythm, a perfect beat.
It dances through the air, so light,
Filling my world with pure delight.
Her hair, like twilight's gentle flow,
A river of silk, with a golden glow.
Each strand a thread of woven light,
In its touch, I find my sight.
Her smile, a dawn that breaks the night,
A beacon of hope, pure and bright.
With every glance, my heart takes flight,
In its glow, my soul ignites.
Her presence, an angelic embrace,
A serene calm, a timeless space.
With her, my spirit finds release,
In her love, eternal peace.

The Light of My Life

Her eyes, a canvas of the skies,
Reflecting depths where my heart lies.
In their gaze, I find my peace,
A moment where my troubles cease.
Her voice, a gentle symphony,
A melody that sets me free.
Each word she speaks, a loving grace,
That fills my heart and lights my face.
Her laughter, a cascade of joy,
A sound so pure, without alloy.
It brightens every corner of my soul,
In its echo, I feel whole.
Her hair, a river of night and gold,
Flowing freely, stories untold.
Each strand, a silken thread of light,
In its flow, I find my sight.
Her smile, a sunrise in my heart,
A glow that never will depart.
With every beam, my spirit lifts,
In its warmth, I find life's gifts.
Her presence, a sanctuary serene,
In her aura, my soul is clean.
A gentle strength, a calming tide,
In her love, I safely bide.

Eternal Allure

Her eyes, a portal to the stars,
In their depths, my heart unbars.
Emerald flames that burn so bright,
Guiding me through darkest night.
Her voice, a lullaby of love,
A gentle coo from skies above.
Each note she sings, a soothing balm,
Wrapping my soul in tender calm.
Her laughter, a ripple in the air,
A joyous sound, beyond compare.
It dances with a light so pure,
In its melody, my heart is sure.
Her hair, a cascade of shimmering light,
Flows with a grace that takes flight.
Each strand, a silken thread of dawn,
In its touch, my love is drawn.
Her smile, a burst of heaven's grace,
Illuminates the darkest place.
With every curve, my spirit soars,
In its glow, my heart adores.
Her presence, a haven of peace,
In her aura, my worries cease.
With her, I find my truest self,
In her love, eternal wealth.

Enchanted Glimpse

Her eyes, like twilight's first embrace,
Reflect a world of endless grace.
In their depths, my heart does see,
A vision of eternity.
Her voice, a melody of spring,
A gentle tune that robins sing.
Each word a note, so pure, so clear,
A song of love, for me to hear.
Her laughter, a symphony of light,
Chasing away the darkest night.
In its joy, my soul finds peace,
A sound where all my troubles cease.
Her hair, like rivers of the dawn,
Flows with beauty, pure and drawn.
Each strand a thread of silken gold,
In its touch, a story told.
Her smile, a beacon bright and true,
Illuminates my every view.
With every curve, my heart does rise,
In its warmth, my spirit flies.
Her presence, a gentle, calming sea,
In her aura, I find me.
A sanctuary where I belong,
In her love, forever strong.

Celestial Beauty

Her eyes, twin stars in the night,
Shine with a celestial light.
In their gaze, I lose my way,
A world where dreams hold sway.
Her voice, a whisper on the breeze,
A lullaby that brings me ease.
Each word a balm, so soft, so sweet,
A melody where our hearts meet.
Her laughter, a cascade of joy,
A sound that no sorrow can destroy.
In its echo, I find my bliss,
A moment of pure happiness.
Her hair, a waterfall of grace,
Flows with elegance, frames her face.
Each strand a wave of silken light,
In its glow, my world turns bright.
Her smile, a sunrise in my soul,
A light that makes me whole.
With every beam, my heart does sing,
In its warmth, I find my spring.
Her presence, a haven pure and still,
In her company, I find my will.
A place of peace, both calm and free,
In her love, my destiny.

Radiant Glow

Her eyes, like windows to the skies,
Reveal a world where my heart lies.
In their depths, a thousand tales,
Of love that never fails.
Her voice, a symphony so grand,
Each note a touch of her hand.
It weaves through air, a magic thread,
A song where dreams are led.
Her laughter, a bell of golden sound,
Spreads joy and light all around.
In its ring, my spirit soars,
A melody that endlessly pours.
Her hair, a river of moonlit night,
Flows with beauty, pure delight.
Each strand a silken, gentle stream,
In its flow, I find my dream.
Her smile, a light that never fades,
Guides me through the darkest shades.
With every glance, my soul does glow,
In its warmth, love's essence flows.
Her presence, a peaceful, gentle breeze,
In her aura, my heart finds ease.
A sanctuary of love and light,
In her embrace, everything feels right.

Timeless Elegance

Her eyes, deep pools of mystery,
Reflect a world of history.
In their depths, I find my place,
A haven of eternal grace.
Her voice, a melody of love,
Soft and gentle, like a dove.
Each word a caress, pure and true,
A song that binds my heart anew.
Her laughter, a joyous chime,
A sound that transcends all time.
In its echo, my worries fade,
A tune of peace, serenely played.
Her hair, a cascade of the night,
Flows with a silken, soft delight.
Each strand a whisper of the dawn,
In its touch, my love is drawn.
Her smile, a beacon in the storm,
Radiates a light so warm.
With every curve, my heart takes flight,
In its glow, I find my light.
Her presence, a calm, serene embrace,
A sanctuary, a sacred space.
In her company, my soul finds peace,
In her love, my dreams increase.

Divine Reflection

In her eyes, the stars align,
A universe in emerald shine.
Each glance she gives, a touch of grace,
In their depths, my heart finds place.
Her voice, a serenade of peace,
A melody where troubles cease.
Each word she speaks, a gentle song,
A hymn where my heart belongs.
Her laughter, a joyous, ringing chime,
A sound that transcends space and time.
In its echo, I find delight,
A melody that makes my soul take flight.
Her hair, a river of twilight's glow,
Flows like a dream, soft and slow.
Each strand, a thread of silken light,
In its touch, my world turns bright.
Her smile, a beacon in the gloom,
A light that banishes all doom.
With every beam, my spirit lifts,
In its glow, I find life's gifts.
Her presence, a calming, sacred space,
A haven of eternal grace.
With her, my soul finds peace,
In her love, my joys increase.

Seraphic Vision

Her eyes, like windows to the skies,
Hold secrets where my heart lies.
In their depths, a tranquil sea,
A world where dreams and love run free.
Her voice, a lullaby so sweet,
A melody where hearts do meet.
Each word she speaks, a tender kiss,
A song of endless, boundless bliss.
Her laughter, a ripple of pure joy,
A sound no sorrow can destroy.
In its echo, my worries fade,
A tune where love is serenely played.
Her hair, a cascade of the dawn,
Flows with beauty, softly drawn.
Each strand a silken, gentle wave,
In its touch, my soul is saved.
Her smile, a ray of morning light,
Chases away the darkest night.
With every curve, my heart does soar,
In its warmth, I yearn for more.
Her presence, an aura of serene,
A place where love and light convene.
In her company, my spirit thrives,
In her love, my essence lives.

Celestial Beauty

Her eyes, a canvas of the night,
Twinkling stars that shine so bright.
In their gaze, I see my fate,
A destiny that love creates.
Her voice, a gentle breeze in spring,
A whisper soft, a song to sing.
Each note she utters, pure and clear,
A melody that draws me near.
Her laughter, a chorus of delight,
A sound that fills my heart with light.
In its echo, joy I find,
A symphony that heals my mind.
Her hair, like waves of golden dawn,
Flows with elegance, softly drawn.
Each strand a silken, gentle ray,
In its touch, my worries sway.
Her smile, a beacon in the dark,
Illuminates my soul's own spark.
With every glance, my heart takes flight,
In its glow, love feels so right.
Her presence, a serene, calming sea,
A sanctuary where I'm free.
With her, my world is pure and true,
In her love, I find my view.

Eternal Elegance

Her eyes, two jewels of endless light,
Hold a universe, pure and bright.
In their depths, my heart does see,
A vision of eternity.
Her voice, a song of gentle grace,
Each word a touch, a warm embrace.
It weaves a spell, so soft, so sweet,
A melody where dreams and reality meet.
Her laughter, a bell of pure delight,
Ringing through the silent night.
In its sound, my worries cease,
A tune of joy, a touch of peace.
Her hair, a cascade of the stars,
Flows like a river, soft and far.
Each strand a silken thread of gold,
In its touch, a story told.
Her smile, a dawn of endless grace,
Lights up the darkest place.
With every beam, my soul does rise,
In its warmth, I find the skies.
Her presence, a gentle, calming air,
A sanctuary, pure and rare.
In her aura, peace I find,
A refuge for my heart and mind.

Eternal Muse

In her eyes, the stars align,
Glistening with a light so fine.
A galaxy within their gaze,
Where dreams and wonders interlace.
Her voice, a symphony of love,
Soft as whispers from above.
Each word she speaks, a tender note,
A lullaby that keeps me afloat.
Her laughter, a melody divine,
A joyful sound, a perfect rhyme.
In its echo, my heart does sing,
A song of happiness it brings.
Her hair, a cascade of the night,
Flowing with a gentle light.
Each strand a silken, moonlit beam,
In its touch, I find my dream.
Her smile, a dawn of endless grace,
Illuminates my darkest place.
With every curve, my spirit flies,
In its warmth, I touch the skies.
Her presence, a haven pure and true,
A sanctuary where I renew.
In her aura, I find peace,
A love that grants my soul release.

Unforgettable Beauty

Her eyes, a masterpiece of art,
Reflecting the depths of her heart.
In their gaze, I lose my way,
A path where love and dreams sway.
Her voice, a gentle, soothing breeze,
A melody that puts my mind at ease.
Each word a touch, so soft and kind,
A song that lingers in my mind.
Her laughter, a joyous serenade,
A sound where happiness is made.
In its ring, my worries cease,
A tune that brings my soul to peace.
Her hair, a river of golden hue,
Flows with grace, pure and true.
Each strand a ray of morning light,
In its glow, my world is bright.
Her smile, a beacon in the storm,
Radiates a light so warm.
With every glance, my heart does soar,
In its shine, I find my core.
Her presence, a tranquil sea,
In her company, I feel free.
A place where love and light reside,
In her embrace, my dreams abide.

Celestial Charm

Her eyes, two stars in a twilight sky,
Sparkling with a love that will never die.
In their depths, a universe untold,
A story of warmth, pure as gold.
Her voice, a hymn of serene delight,
A gentle whisper through the night.
Each word she speaks, a soothing breeze,
A melody that puts my heart at ease.
Her laughter, a radiant, joyous sound,
Fills the air, all around.
In its echo, I find pure bliss,
A melody I cannot miss.
Her hair, a silken waterfall,
Flows like a dream, over all.
Each strand a touch of golden light,
In its shimmer, everything feels right.
Her smile, a sunrise breaking through,
A light that makes the world anew.
With every beam, my soul does rise,
In its warmth, I reach the skies.
Her presence, a serene, calming grace,
A sanctuary, a sacred space.
In her aura, I find peace,
A love that grants my heart release.

Infinite Grace

Her eyes, like portals to the stars,
Hold a world beyond all scars.
In their gaze, I see my fate,
A destiny that love creates.
Her voice, a tender lullaby,
A gentle tune that never dies.
Each note she utters, pure and clear,
A song that draws me ever near.
Her laughter, a chime of pure delight,
A sound that fills my heart with light.
In its echo, joy I find,
A symphony that heals my mind.
Her hair, like waves of golden dawn,
Flows with beauty, softly drawn.
Each strand a silken, gentle ray,
In its touch, my worries sway.
Her smile, a beacon in the night,
Illuminates my soul's own light.
With every glance, my heart takes flight,
In its glow, love feels so right.
Her presence, a sanctuary serene,
A place where love and light convene.
In her company, my spirit thrives,
In her love, my essence lives.

Starry Eyes

Her eyes, a universe so grand,
In their depths, a world unplanned.
Twinkling stars in the night sky,
Where hopes and dreams do not shy.
Her voice, a whisper in the breeze,
A lullaby that sets me at ease.
Each word, a note of purest love,
Descending like a dove from above.
Her laughter, a melody so sweet,
A symphony where joy and light meet.
In its echo, I find my place,
A tune that fills the empty space.
Her hair, a cascade of the moon,
Flowing with a silken tune.
Each strand a whisper of the night,
In its touch, everything feels right.
Her smile, a dawn of pure delight,
Illuminates my darkest night.
With every beam, my soul takes flight,
In its glow, my heart is light.
Her presence, a serene, sacred space,
A haven of love, a gentle grace.
With her, my world is complete,
In her love, I find my beat.

Heavenly Grace

Her eyes, two pools of liquid light,
Shining with a grace so bright.
In their depths, I see the stars,
A glimpse of heaven, near and far.
Her voice, a melody so fine,
A symphony of the divine.
Each word she speaks, a gentle tone,
A song that makes me feel at home.
Her laughter, a ripple of delight,
A sound that turns the dark to light.
In its echo, joy I find,
A melody that soothes my mind.
Her hair, a river of golden streams,
Flowing with the light of dreams.
Each strand a silken, soft caress,
In its touch, I find my rest.
Her smile, a beacon in the storm,
Radiates a light so warm.
With every curve, my heart does soar,
In its glow, I yearn for more.
Her presence, a tranquil, calming sea,
A sanctuary where I'm free.
In her aura, peace I find,
A love that lifts my heart and mind.

Eternal Allure

Her eyes, a mirror of the stars,
Reflecting a universe without scars.
In their gaze, I see my dream,
A world where love is the theme.
Her voice, a lullaby of peace,
A melody where troubles cease.
Each note she sings, a gentle kiss,
A song of endless, boundless bliss.
Her laughter, a bell of golden sound,
Spreads joy and light all around.
In its echo, my worries fade,
A tune where love serenely played.
Her hair, a cascade of silken threads,
Flows like rivers over beds.
Each strand, a ray of morning light,
In its touch, everything feels right.
Her smile, a sunrise in my soul,
A light that makes me whole.
With every glance, my spirit lifts,
In its glow, I find life's gifts.
Her presence, a serene, gentle air,
A sanctuary, pure and fair.
With her, my soul finds peace,
In her love, my dreams increase.

Serene Elegance

Her eyes, like orbs of emerald fire,
Sparkle with a pure desire.
In their depths, I lose my way,
A place where night turns to day.
Her voice, a gentle song of love,
Soft and tender as a dove.
Each word a touch, so sweet and kind,
A melody that fills my mind.
Her laughter, a joyous, ringing chime,
A sound that transcends all time.
In its echo, joy I find,
A symphony that heals my mind.
Her hair, a river of silken night,
Flows with a grace that's pure delight.
Each strand, a whisper of the dawn,
In its touch, my love is drawn.
Her smile, a beacon in the dark,
Illuminates my soul's own spark.
With every beam, my heart does rise,
In its warmth, I find the skies.
Her presence, a gentle, calming sea,
In her aura, I feel free.
A sanctuary of love and light,
In her embrace, everything feels right.

Timeless Elegance

Her eyes, a canvas of the skies,
Hold a world where love resides.
In their gaze, I find my peace,
A moment where all troubles cease.
Her voice, a serenade of grace,
A melody that time can't erase.
Each word she speaks, a note so sweet,
A song that makes my heart complete.
Her laughter, a cascade of delight,
A sound that turns the dark to light.
In its echo, my spirit soars,
A tune that I forever adore.
Her hair, a waterfall of grace,
Flows like a dream, soft and traced.
Each strand, a silken, gentle thread,
In its touch, my heart is led.
Her smile, a dawn that breaks the night,
A beacon of hope, pure and bright.
With every curve, my soul does rise,
In its glow, I reach the skies.
Her presence, a serene, calming space,
A sanctuary of endless grace.
With her, my world is pure and true,
In her love, I find my view.

Infinite Radiance

Her eyes, a mirror of the night,
Twinkle with a starry light.
In their depths, I see the skies,
A universe where my heart lies.
Her voice, a breeze of summer's eve,
A melody that makes me believe.
Each word she speaks, a soft caress,
A song that fills my heart with bliss.
Her laughter, a joyous, gentle ring,
A sound where happiness does spring.
In its echo, I find my peace,
A tune where all my sorrows cease.
Her hair, like waves of twilight gold,
Flows with stories yet untold.
Each strand a thread of silken light,
In its touch, the world feels right.
Her smile, a sunrise in the morn,
A glow that makes my soul reborn.
With every curve, my spirit flies,
In its warmth, I reach the skies.
Her presence, a haven calm and bright,
A sanctuary in the night.
With her, my world is full and free,
In her love, I find my key.

Celestial Glow

Her eyes, a canvas of the dawn,
In their depths, my dreams are drawn.
Twinkling with a light so rare,
A universe beyond compare.
Her voice, a whisper in the night,
A melody of pure delight.
Each word she speaks, a gentle breeze,
A song that puts my heart at ease.
Her laughter, a ripple in the air,
A sound so sweet, beyond compare.
In its echo, joy I find,
A symphony that soothes my mind.
Her hair, a cascade of moonlit streams,
Flows with the light of my dreams.
Each strand a silken, gentle ray,
In its touch, my worries sway.
Her smile, a beacon pure and true,
Illuminates my every view.
With every glance, my heart does rise,
In its glow, I touch the skies.
Her presence, a calm, serene embrace,
A sanctuary of endless grace.
In her aura, I find peace,
A love that grants my soul release.

Eternal Light

Her eyes, like stars that light the sky,
Glimmer with a love so high.
In their gaze, I lose my way,
A world where night turns into day.
Her voice, a melody of spring,
A gentle tune that robins sing.
Each word she speaks, a tender kiss,
A song of love, eternal bliss.
Her laughter, a joyous, ringing bell,
A sound where happiness does dwell.
In its echo, I find my cheer,
A tune that brings my soul near.
Her hair, a river of the night,
Flows with a soft, gentle light.
Each strand a thread of silken gold,
In its touch, a story told.
Her smile, a dawn of endless grace,
Illuminates my darkest place.
With every curve, my heart does soar,
In its warmth, I yearn for more.
Her presence, a haven calm and pure,
A place where love is sure.
With her, my world is right and true,
In her love, my dreams come through.

Heavenly Radiance

Her eyes, like gems of the night,
Sparkle with a radiant light.
In their depths, I find my dreams,
A place where love flows in streams.
Her voice, a whisper soft and kind,
A melody that fills my mind.
Each word she speaks, a gentle breeze,
A song that puts my heart at ease.
Her laughter, a joyous, tender sound,
Fills the air and all around.
In its echo, my spirit soars,
A tune that I forever adore.
Her hair, like rivers of the dawn,
Flows with grace, softly drawn.
Each strand a silken, gentle wave,
In its touch, my soul is saved.
Her smile, a beacon in the night,
Guides me with its gentle light.
With every glance, my heart takes flight,
In its glow, I find my sight.
Her presence, a serene, calming sea,
A sanctuary where I'm free.
In her aura, peace I find,
A love that lifts my heart and mind.

Divine Light

Her eyes, a pair of twinkling stars,
Hold a universe without bars.
In their gaze, I see my fate,
A destiny that love creates.
Her voice, a tender lullaby,
A melody that makes me sigh.
Each note she sings, a touch of grace,
A song that takes me to a special place.
Her laughter, a melody so fine,
A symphony of love divine.
In its echo, my heart does cheer,
A tune that draws my soul near.
Her hair, a waterfall of light,
Flows with a grace that's pure delight.
Each strand, a silken, gentle ray,
In its touch, I find my way.
Her smile, a dawn of purest gold,
Lights up stories yet untold.
With every curve, my spirit lifts,
In its warmth, I find life's gifts.
Her presence, a serene, gentle air,
A sanctuary, pure and fair.
In her company, I find my rest,
In her love, I am truly blessed.

Celestial Radiance

Her eyes, like twin orbs of light,
Illuminate the darkest night.
In their depths, I find my peace,
A love that never will cease.
Her voice, a gentle, soothing tune,
Soft as a whisper under the moon.
Each word a melody, sweet and pure,
A song of love that will endure.
Her laughter, a joyous, ringing bell,
A sound where happiness does dwell.
In its echo, I find my joy,
A tune that nothing can destroy.
Her hair, like waves of twilight gold,
Flows with stories yet untold.
Each strand a silken, gentle light,
In its touch, my heart feels right.
Her smile, a beacon bright and true,
Lights up my world, makes everything new.
With every curve, my soul takes flight,
In its warmth, my spirit is light.
Her presence, a serene, calming sea,
A sanctuary where I'm free.
In her aura, peace I find,
A love that lifts my heart and mind.

Timeless Beauty

Her eyes, a portal to the skies,
Hold a world where love lies.
In their depths, I lose my way,
A place where night turns to day.
Her voice, a symphony of spring,
A gentle tune that angels sing.
Each word she speaks, a tender kiss,
A melody of eternal bliss.
Her laughter, a joyous, ringing chime,
A sound that transcends all time.
In its echo, my spirit soars,
A tune that I forever adore.
Her hair, a river of silken night,
Flows with grace, pure delight.
Each strand a whisper of the dawn,
In its touch, my love is drawn.
Her smile, a dawn of endless grace,
Illuminates my darkest place.
With every beam, my heart does rise,
In its warmth, I find the skies.
Her presence, a serene, calming air,
A sanctuary, pure and fair.
With her, my soul finds peace,
In her love, my dreams increase.

Ethereal Glow

Her eyes, two stars in a twilight sky,
Gleam with a love that will not die.
In their depths, I see my dreams,
A world where love flows in streams.
Her voice, a whisper in the breeze,
A melody that sets me at ease.
Each word a touch of softest grace,
A song that takes me to a special place.
Her laughter, a bell of pure delight,
A sound that turns the dark to light.
In its echo, joy I find,
A melody that heals my mind.
Her hair, a waterfall of gold,
Flows with beauty, pure and bold.
Each strand a silken, gentle wave,
In its touch, my soul is saved.
Her smile, a sunrise breaking through,
A light that makes the world anew.
With every curve, my heart does soar,
In its glow, I yearn for more.
Her presence, a haven calm and bright,
A sanctuary in the night.
With her, my world is right and true,
In her love, I find my view.

Angelic Vision

Her eyes, like pools of liquid light,
Shine with a grace so pure and bright.
In their depths, I see the stars,
A universe without any bars.
Her voice, a melody of love,
Soft and gentle as a dove.
Each word she speaks, a lullaby,
A song that makes my heart sigh.
Her laughter, a joyous, ringing bell,
A sound where happiness does dwell.
In its echo, joy I find,
A tune that lingers in my mind.
Her hair, a river of twilight streams,
Flows with the light of my dreams.
Each strand a silken, gentle ray,
In its touch, my worries sway.
Her smile, a beacon in the dark,
Illuminates my soul's own spark.
With every glance, my heart does rise,
In its warmth, I touch the skies.
Her presence, a serene, calming sea,
A sanctuary where I'm free.
With her, my world is full and bright,
In her love, I find my light.

Seraphic Light

Her eyes, like jewels in the night,
Sparkle with a pure delight.
In their gaze, I find my way,
A path where love will always stay.
Her voice, a melody of peace,
A gentle tune where worries cease.
Each word she speaks, a tender kiss,
A song of endless, boundless bliss.
Her laughter, a symphony of joy,
A sound that no sorrow can destroy.
In its echo, my spirit soars,
A melody that I adore.
Her hair, like waves of golden dawn,
Flows with a grace that's softly drawn.
Each strand a silken, gentle thread,
In its touch, my heart is led.
Her smile, a light in the storm,
Radiates a warmth so warm.
With every curve, my soul takes flight,
In its glow, everything is right.
Her presence, a haven of calm,
A sanctuary, a healing balm.
With her, my world is pure and true,
In her love, I find my view.

Enchanted Eyes

Her eyes, a canvas of the night,
Sparkle with a mystical light.
In their gaze, I find my dreams,
A world where love flows in streams.
Her voice, a lullaby so sweet,
A melody that makes me complete.
Each word she speaks, a tender kiss,
A song that fills my heart with bliss.
Her laughter, a joyous, gentle chime,
A sound that transcends all time.
In its echo, my soul does soar,
A tune that I forever adore.
Her hair, a river of silken gold,
Flows with stories yet untold.
Each strand a whisper of delight,
In its touch, the world feels right.
Her smile, a sunrise in my soul,
A light that makes me whole.
With every curve, my heart takes flight,
In its warmth, my spirit is light.
Her presence, a serene, calming sea,
A sanctuary where I'm free.
With her, my world is pure and bright,
In her love, I find my light.

Serene Beauty

Her eyes, like windows to the stars,
Gleam with a light that heals all scars.
In their depths, I find my peace,
A love that will never cease.
Her voice, a melody so fine,
A gentle tune that is divine.
Each word she speaks, a gentle breeze,
A song that puts my heart at ease.
Her laughter, a symphony of joy,
A sound that no sorrow can destroy.
In its echo, I find my cheer,
A melody that draws me near.
Her hair, a cascade of silken night,
Flows with a grace that's pure delight.
Each strand a ray of morning light,
In its touch, everything feels right.
Her smile, a beacon in the dark,
Illuminates my soul's own spark.
With every glance, my heart does rise,
In its glow, I touch the skies.
Her presence, a tranquil, calming air,
A sanctuary pure and fair.
With her, my soul finds peace,
In her love, my dreams increase.

Eternal Allure

Her eyes, a mirror of the stars,
Reflecting a universe without scars.
In their gaze, I see my fate,
A destiny that love creates.
Her voice, a gentle, soothing tone,
A melody that makes me feel at home.
Each word she speaks, a tender note,
A song that keeps my heart afloat.
Her laughter, a joyous, ringing sound,
Fills the air all around.
In its echo, I find my joy,
A tune that nothing can destroy.
Her hair, a river of the night,
Flows with a soft, gentle light.
Each strand a thread of silken gold,
In its touch, a story told.
Her smile, a dawn of endless grace,
Illuminates my darkest place.
With every curve, my heart does soar,
In its warmth, I yearn for more.
Her presence, a serene, calming space,
A sanctuary of endless grace.
With her, my world is right and true,
In her love, I find my view.

Divine Grace

Her eyes, like stars that light the sky,
Gleam with a love that will never die.
In their gaze, I lose my way,
A path where night turns to day.
Her voice, a melody so sweet,
A gentle tune that makes me complete.
Each word she speaks, a soft caress,
A song that fills my heart with bliss.
Her laughter, a joyous, ringing chime,
A sound that transcends all time.
In its echo, my spirit soars,
A tune that I forever adore.
Her hair, a river of golden streams,
Flows with the light of my dreams.
Each strand a silken, gentle wave,
In its touch, my soul is saved.
Her smile, a beacon in the night,
Radiates a light so bright.
With every curve, my heart does rise,
In its glow, I touch the skies.
Her presence, a haven calm and pure,
A place where love is sure.
With her, my world is full and bright,
In her love, I find my light.

Celestial Charm

Her eyes, like orbs of emerald fire,
Sparkle with a pure desire.
In their gaze, I see the skies,
A universe where my heart lies.
Her voice, a gentle song of love,
Soft and tender as a dove.
Each word a touch, so sweet and kind,
A melody that fills my mind.
Her laughter, a joyous, ringing sound,
Fills the air and all around.
In its echo, I find my cheer,
A tune that brings my soul near.
Her hair, a cascade of the moon,
Flowing with a silken tune.
Each strand a whisper of delight,
In its touch, everything feels right.
Her smile, a sunrise in my soul,
A light that makes me whole.
With every beam, my spirit flies,
In its warmth, I reach the skies.
Her presence, a serene, gentle air,
A sanctuary, pure and fair.
With her, my soul finds peace,
In her love, my dreams increase.

Heavenly Radiance

Her eyes, like pools of liquid light,
Shine with a grace so pure and bright.
In their depths, I see the stars,
A universe without any bars.
Her voice, a melody of love,
Soft and gentle as a dove.
Each word she speaks, a lullaby,
A song that makes my heart sigh.
Her laughter, a joyous, ringing bell,
A sound where happiness does dwell.
In its echo, joy I find,
A tune that lingers in my mind.
Her hair, a river of twilight streams,
Flows with the light of my dreams.
Each strand a silken, gentle ray,
In its touch, my worries sway.
Her smile, a beacon in the dark,
Illuminates my soul's own spark.
With every glance, my heart does rise,
In its warmth, I touch the skies.
Her presence, a serene, calming sea,
A sanctuary where I'm free.
With her, my world is pure and bright,
In her love, I find my light.

Eternal Radiance

In her eyes, a universe unfurled,
A symphony of stars, a cosmic swirl.
Her gaze, a beacon in the night,
Guiding me with its radiant light.
Each word she speaks, a melody rare,
A song of love that fills the air.
Her voice, a whisper soft and clear,
A soothing balm to calm my fear.
Her laughter, a chorus of delight,
A melody that ignites the night.
In its echo, my worries flee,
Replaced by joy and serenity.
Her smile, a sunrise in my heart,
A glow that sets my soul apart.
With every beam, my spirit soars,
In its warmth, my love restores.
Her presence, a sanctuary pure,
A haven where my soul feels sure.
With her, I find my eternal dance,
In her love, I find my true romance.

Soul's Symphony

In her eyes, a melody divine,
A universe where stars align.
Each glance, a note of sweet refrain,
A song of love that knows no pain.
Her voice, a sonnet soft and true,
A serenade that pulls me through.
Each word, a verse of pure delight,
A melody that fills my night.
Her laughter, a chorus in the air,
A symphony beyond compare.
In its echo, my heart takes flight,
A tune that lifts me to new heights.
Her smile, a crescendo of bliss,
A radiant beam I cannot miss.
With every curve, my soul is stirred,
In its glow, my love is heard.
Her presence, a harmony complete,
A melody that makes life sweet.
With her, my heart finds its key,
In her love, I am truly free.

Eternal Echoes

In her eyes, a universe untold,
A symphony of love, pure gold.
Each glance, a whisper in the night,
A melody that fills me with delight.
Her voice, a gentle breeze's sigh,
A serenade that lifts me high.
Each word, a verse of endless grace,
A song of love that finds its place.
Her laughter, a melody divine,
A chorus in this heart of mine.
In its echo, my soul takes flight,
A tune that brings me pure delight.
Her smile, a beacon in the dark,
A light that guides me like a spark.
With every curve, my spirit sings,
In its glow, my heart takes wings.
Her presence, a symphony complete,
A harmony that makes life sweet.
With her, I find my truest song,
In her love, I belong.

Infinite Serenity

In her eyes, a tranquil sea,
Where love and light forever be.
Each glance, a wave of pure delight,
A beacon in the darkest night.
Her voice, a melody so sweet,
A symphony that can't be beat.
Each word, a note of endless grace,
A song that fills this empty space.
Her laughter, a gentle breeze,
A melody that brings me ease.
In its echo, my worries fade,
A tune that brings the serenade.
Her smile, a sunrise in my heart,
A light that never will depart.
With every curve, my soul does soar,
In its glow, I find much more.
Her presence, a sanctuary divine,
A place where truest love does shine.
With her, my world is pure and free,
In her love, I find eternity.

Whispers of Eternity

In her eyes, a universe unfolds,
Where love's story forever molds.
Each glance, a whispered promise made,
In the quiet moments, love displayed.
Her voice, a soft and tender breeze,
That brings my restless soul at ease.
Each word, a melody of truth,
In the symphony of love's sweet youth.
Her laughter, a melody of joy,
That fills my heart without alloy.
In its echo, I find my home,
Wherever she may choose to roam.
Her smile, a beacon in the night,
Guiding me through shadows' blight.
With every curve, my heart is stirred,
By the beauty of her every word.
Her presence, a haven of grace,
Where I find my rightful place.
In her love, I find my serenity,
In her arms, whispers of eternity.

Celestial Melodies

In her eyes, constellations gleam,
A celestial dance in a cosmic stream.
Each glance, a starburst of desire,
Igniting passions that never tire.
Her voice, a symphony of the spheres,
Resonating through my deepest fears.
Each word, a note in love's grand score,
A melody that leaves me wanting more.
Her laughter, a chorus of delight,
Echoing through the endless night.
In its resonance, my spirit soars,
To heights unknown, to distant shores.
Her smile, a radiant aurora's glow,
Illuminating paths I used to not know.
With every curve, my heart takes flight,
In its warmth, everything feels right.
Her presence, a celestial embrace,
A sanctuary in time and space.
In her love, I find my sanctuary,
In her arms, celestial melodies.

Eternal Harmony

In her eyes, galaxies unfurl,
A cosmic dance, a wondrous swirl.
Each glance, a glimpse of paradise,
Where love and dreams harmonize.
Her voice, a symphony divine,
Echoing through the stars aligned.
Each word, a note of purest grace,
In the symphony of love's embrace.
Her laughter, a celestial choir,
Filling the night with love's fire.
In its echo, my spirit sings,
As joy through the universe rings.
Her smile, a beacon in the dark,
Guiding me to love's true spark.
With every curve, my soul takes flight,
In its glow, I find endless light.
Her presence, a celestial symphony,
A harmony of love's eternity.
In her embrace, I find my home,
Where love and peace forever roam.

Infinite Bliss

In her eyes, a universe of dreams,
Where love flows in eternal streams.
Each glance, a glimpse of paradise,
Where hearts dance beneath starlit skies.
Her voice, a melody so sweet,
Guiding me through life's retreat.
Each word, a verse of endless grace,
In the symphony of love's embrace.
Her laughter, a melody divine,
Echoing through the endless line.
In its echo, my spirit soars,
As joy fills the universe's shores.
Her smile, a beacon in the night,
Guiding me with its radiant light.
With every curve, my soul takes flight,
In its warmth, everything feels right.
Her presence, a sanctuary serene,
A haven where love's purest sheen.
In her embrace, I find my bliss,
Lost in the eternity of her kiss.

Divine Embrace

In her eyes, the stars align,
A universe where love intertwine.
Each glance, a journey to the divine,
Where souls entwine, hearts combine.
Her voice, a melody so pure,
Guiding me through life's allure.
Each word, a verse of endless grace,
In the symphony of love's embrace.
Her laughter, a chorus of delight,
Echoing through the endless night.
In its echo, my worries cease,
As love's harmony brings peace.
Her smile, a beacon in the dark,
Guiding me to love's true spark.
With every curve, my spirit flies,
In its glow, my heart lies.
Her presence, a sanctuary of love,
A haven where souls soar above.
In her arms, I find my place,
Lost in the beauty of her embrace.

About the Author

Mrigendra Bharti, born on June 29, 2004, in South Delhi, India, is a multifaceted individual recognized as the owner of Mrigendra Bharti Group InfoTech India Co. Pvt Ltd. Beyond his entrepreneurial endeavors, he is a distinguished music producer, director, and a budding writer.

Embarking on his professional journey at a young age, Mrigendra Bharti's visionary leadership has led to the establishment of several successful ventures, including Croma Music Series Entertainment, Sellbrochure, Fauget Innovative, and more.

What sets Mrigendra apart is his early initiation into the world of business. His foray into the unknown realms of entrepreneurship began during his 10th-grade years, where he delved into the music industry. This initial venture laid the foundation for subsequent achievements, showcasing his dedication and resilience.

Having honed his skills in music, Mrigendra Bharti not only demonstrated significant growth in his craft but also expanded his professional network. His passion extends beyond music, encompassing app and website development, as well as graphic design.

Fueled by his creative aspirations, Mrigendra established the Mrigendra Bharti Group, a company specializing in website and app development. Currently, he collaborates with a dedicated team, collectively working on ambitious projects that promise innovation and excellence.

Mrigendra's journey serves as an inspiration, particularly for today's students, highlighting the potential of youthful determination and the ability to transform innovative ideas into successful businesses. As he continues to make strides in various domains, Mrigendra Bharti remains a dynamic force, contributing vibrancy to the realms of business, music, and technology.

Read more at https://www.imwriter-mrigendra.rf.gd.